SUFFOLK COAST
FROM THE AIR

SUFFOLK COAST
FROM THE AIR

Mike Page & Pauline Young

HALSGROVE

First published in Great Britain in 2006
Reprinted February 2007, Reprinted May 2007
Copyright © 2006 photographs Mike Page
Copyright © 2006 text Pauline Young

British Library Cataloguing-in-Publication Data
A CIP record for this title is available from the British Library

ISBN 978 1 84114 572 3

HALSGROVE
Halsgrove House
Ryelands Farm Industrial Estate
Bagley Green, Wellington
Somerset TA21 9PZ
Tel: 01823 653777
Fax: 01823 665294
email: sales@halsgrove.com
website: www.halsgrove.com

Printed and bound by D'Auria Industrie Grafiche Spa, Italy

FOREWORD

Mike Page's intimate knowledge of the area and his interest in flying and photography make him particularly well qualified to create this fine collection of aerial pictures of Suffolk's coastline.

Geography has bequeathed the county with an isolation that has shaped its great character. And its scenery is delightful, as you'll see.

The seaside towns, major and minor ports, fishing villages, woodlands, nature reserves and seaside resorts show off their character so well.

Long gone are the brigands and pirates who dominated this coastline in yesteryear. Its constant domination continues to be the North Sea which shapes the coastline and keeps it in a state of change.

You'll enjoy these outstanding bird's-eye views of Suffolk's fine coastline and Pauline Young's excellent accompanying text notes.

James Hoseason OBE

ACKNOWLEDGEMENTS

Our thanks go to the many individuals and organisations who have helped with the information contained in this book, but particularly to Roy Snelling, Bob Malster, Gerry Parsons, Keith Atkins, Keith Nunn, Alec Watson, James Hoseason OBE, Judy Speed, Derek Edwards, the RSPB, Air Traffic Control at Norwich Airport and fellow co-pilots Brian Barr and Peter Day from Seething Airfield, Norfolk.

And, of course, our thanks to our spouses Gillian Page and John Young for putting up with our preoccupation throughout the preparation of this book.

Mike Page, Strumpshaw
Pauline Young, Norwich
2006

DEDICATION

This book is dedicated to the father I never knew, Royal Arthur John Watson Page. He was acting temporary skipper on Minesweeper HMS *Fir* when, in December 1942, he saved the lives of the crew around him by picking up a live grenade that had fallen from a canister on to the deck. It exploded as he threw it overboard and he died shortly afterwards from the injuries he sustained. I was two years old. One of the photographs in this book is of trawler *Excelsior* and as I was flying overhead it reminded me that my father, coming from a fishing family, had served on these ketches and had risen through the ranks to be skipper before the Second World War. I decided at this point to dedicate this book to him.

Michael John Page

INTRODUCTION

Following the success of *Norfolk Coast from the Air* it was decided to make a companion volume of the Suffolk Coastline. The Suffolk coast is very different in character to Norfolk's, mainly because of the abundance of its small harbours and rivers. And because of the scarcity of coastal roads it has in some parts a wildness and isolation hard to find elsewhere.

My cameras are a Canon 1D Mk2 digital with a 80-200 2.8L lens and a Canon 5D with a 24-105 L lens. An ideal combination for aerial photography. Because my camera is hand held I often need to use fast shutter speeds to counter any turbulence. The ideal aircraft is a high wing Cessna 150 which I fly with the window open. A safety pilot accompanies me to keep a lookout and fly the aircraft whilst I'm taking the pictures. My library consists of over 30 000 images stored on computer. I have worked with Pauline Young many times. I began by providing aerial illustrations and still photographs for her magazine articles, then we moved on to aerial videos and books.

All royalties from the sale of this, as with our other films and books, will go to charity. We hope you enjoy this one.

Mike Page

Also by Mike Page and Pauline Young:
A Broads-Eye View Halsgrove 2005
Norfolk Coast from the Air Halsgrove 2006

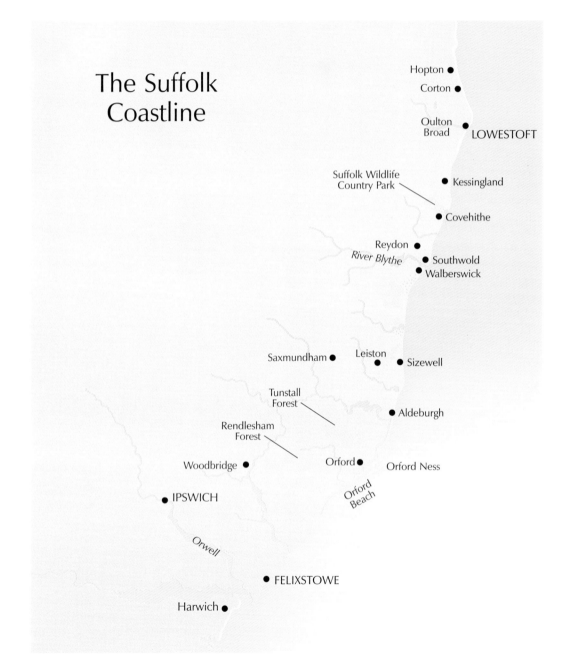

The Suffolk Coastline

Hopton ●

Corton ●

Oulton
Broad ●
LOWESTOFT

Suffolk Wildlife
Country Park
● Kessingland

● Covehithe

Reydon ●
River Blythe
● Southwold
● Walberswick

Saxmundham ●
Leiston ●
● Sizewell

Tunstall
Forest
● Aldeburgh

Rendlesham
Forest

Woodbridge ●
Orford ●
Orford Ness

● IPSWICH
*Orford
Beach*

Orwell

● FELIXSTOWE

Harwich ●

The end of the Stour Navigation

The main Norwich to London railway line (mid picture) crosses the curiously named Cattawade Creek (literally 'cat's ford'). The River Stour, pronounced 'stoor', flows into Harwich Harbour and mingles with the waters of the River Orwell before they empty into the North Sea. In Daniel Defoe's 1794 *Travel through the Eastern Counties* he writes that he chose to travel by boat up to Ipswich but sent his horses via Cataway (his spelling) Bridge.

Between the Stour and the Orwell

The imposing buildings of the Royal Hospital School sit comfortably in the Suffolk countryside with Holbrook village behind and Alton Water Reservoir to the left. The reservoir provides freshwater for Ipswich and the surrounding area and was created in the 1960s on largely agricultural land. The magnificent Orwell Bridge is visible on the horizon. The north bank of the River Stour is in the foreground.

Royal Hospital School

The school moved to this purpose-built site at Holbrook from the Queens House, Greenwich in 1933. It was part of the Greenwich Hospital founded there in 1694 by monarchs William and Mary. Intended originally for the sons of seafarers it is today open to all successful candidates between the ages of 11 and 18 and is coeducational and independent. Until the 1950s boys were required upon leaving to join the Royal or Merchant Navies. This new site was part of the country estate of tea merchant Gifford Sherman Reade who gifted his lands and most of his fortune to the Admiralty in gratitude for the fact that not one of his ships was lost during the First World War. The landmark stone spire stands above the Assembly Hall. Alton Water is in the background.

Shotley Peninsula

King Alfred fought the Vikings here in AD885. Bloody Point near Shotley Marina takes its name from the battle site and is Anglo Saxon for 'a wild empty space'. Two Martello Towers are on the higher ground commanding a good view of an approaching enemy. The towers – named from the Watch Tower at Mortella Point, Corsica (note the slightly different spelling) were built in a chain along the south and east coasts as a counter to the threat of Napoleonic invasion – except that by the time they were completed the threat was non existent! The seventy-four towers stretched in a line from Seaford in Sussex to Aldeburgh in Suffolk. HMS *Ganges*, a three decker training ship, was moored here in the Stour Estuary in 1899 as a Royal Navy training ship. It later moved to a shore establishment until 1976. The 'Mast Manning Ceremony' involved young sailors climbing a 143' mast with one of them standing on the top 11" wide 'button' to give a salute. The *Ganges* regime was said to be very strict. First World War casualties were buried in the Naval Cemetery within Shotley Churchyard, being pulled there on gun carriages. Buried there too are the boys from HMS *Ganges* who died in the 1918 influenza epidemic.

The River Stour looking upriver

Towards the end of the nineteenth century the port of Harwich had become so congested that a new one was created on reclaimed land and named Parkeston Quay, after Charles Parkes chairman of the Great Eastern Railway. The GER, which had financed the project, was an amalgamation of several East Anglian railways. Today the quay is a busy passenger ferry terminal recently renamed Harwich International Port. It serves the continental ferry ports as well as being a cruise departure point. After the First World War one hundred and fifty U-boats surrendered in the River Stour. The high speed ferry to the Hook of Holland is mid picture left. Shotley stands on the opposite bank. The whole Suffolk Coast from the mouth of the Stour to Kessingland has been declared an Area of Outstanding Natural Beauty. The river is the boundary between Suffolk and Essex.

The port of Ipswich

By the seventh century Ipswich was a thriving port trading with the countries on the opposite side of the North Sea. It was given its charter by King John and by 1520 had become England's 6th richest town. In the boom after the Napoleonic Wars the port grew to handle the expanded grain and malt trades. The Wet Dock uses part of the river and was opened in 1842. The coming of the railway in the 1840s increased the town's prosperity and population still further. Very large ships have draughts too deep to navigate the River Orwell which led to the growth of Felixstowe Container Terminal downriver, but Ipswich still is a port with the West Bank Terminal handling RoRo cargo.

The port viewed from above the Orwell Bridge

Thames barges were built here and return to race each June. Ipswich's famous sons include Cardinal Thomas Wolsey, who fell out with Henry VIII over a divorce (Henry's), Thomas Cavendish (the second man to circumnavigate the earth so he shares the same fate of oblivion with the second man to land on the moon), and Geoffrey Chaucer who takes his surname from his wine-importer father Robert le Chaucer – who brought in chausses (casks) of wine from Spain in the fourteenth century. Writer George Orwell was *not* born within thousands of miles of the river from which he took his name *nor* was his name George Orwell, but Eric Blair. Why he chose the pseudonym is a mystery. However he does have a Suffolk connection as his parents lived in Southwold for a time. The pylon has wires stretching across the river because on the opposite bank stood the Cliff Quay Power Station. Ostrich Creek goes off to the left; the Ostrich was on the crest of the first Lord Justice, Lord Coke of nearby Wherstead Manor (1612), but the 'Ostrich' pub has since been renamed the 'Oyster Reach'.

The River Orwell looking towards Felixstowe

The magnificent Orwell Bridge, built 1982, has a 600' centre span of pre-stressed concrete, the longest in the world. Its nineteen sets of concrete piers bore one hundred and twenty feet into the ground and the bridge took three years to build. Felixstowe and the expanse of Harwich Harbour are in the distance. The two red-hulled boats are former Aberdeen trawlers moored at the Sewage Works jetty (off picture). They're brightly coloured because previously they'd been used as North Sea oil rig standby vessels. The bridge forms part of the Ipswich bypass A14 road.

Pin Mill

The 'Butt and Oyster' pub floods regularly on high spring tides and sailors tell of being able to sail their boats right up to the window to place their orders. A butt is a flat fish, as in halibut.

Opposite: **Pin Mill looking towards Felixstowe**

Pin (from pynd or pond) Mill is one of the best known anchorages along the River Orwell. Hulks of old sailing barges and other craft lie on the mud but each summer sees Thames barge races in Harwich Harbour and along the Orwell at Pin Mill. Arthur Ransome for some years lived on the opposite river bank at Levington. He had a boat built at Pin Mill and used the location in his story *We Didn't Mean to go to Sea*. The 'Butt and Oyster' is the large cream-washed building at the water's edge and has been there for several hundred years.

Marina at Levington looking towards Ipswich

For those who prefer gardening to sailing (there's hardly ever time or inclination to do both!), Levington is best known for its soil composts, but the Suffolk Yacht Harbour is popular with sailors from either side of the North Sea. Trading barges once worked along the now dried up Levington Creek. There's evidence of settlement at Levington from Anglo Saxon times. Woolverstone and Pin Mill are on the promontory top left. The red-painted craft is the former Cromer Lightship, now the clubhouse of the Haven Ports Yacht Club.

Harwich Harbour and the Stour and Orwell Estuaries

Felixstowe Container Terminal is bounded on one side by Landguard Point and on the other by Trimley Marshes which belong to the Suffolk Wildlife Trust. The area was taken into the Trust to prevent further enlargement of Felixstowe Docks. The port of Harwich is on the opposite side of the harbour looking across the River Stour to Shotley.

The port of Felixstowe

When St Felix landed here to bring Christianity to the heathen, little did he imagine what the area would look like centuries later. This is the largest container port in Britain and the fourth largest in Europe. In 1967 165 metres of purpose-built container quay at the Landguard Container terminal was opened, the first port in the UK to introduce computerised Customs Clearance. By 1986 the quay had grown to 1½ miles. The port of Felixstowe was begun in 1875 by the Felixstowe Dock and Railway Company. During the First World War it was requisitioned as a Royal Navy Destroyer and Minesweeper base and in the Second World War held Motor Torpedo boats. The town of Felixstowe is in the background.

Colourful Containers

Landguard Point

The tall white tower of the port's radar stands in a local Nature Reserve which has SSSI status. The bird sanctuary is the first point of land for exhausted migratory birds. Seaplanes based at the Felixstowe Air Station were moored at a floating dock in the harbour and this was the main seaplane testing centre. The Schneider Trophy teams formed up here 1927–31, the race was for the fastest seaplane on a closed circuit. Landguard Fort was well named. It was built in the sixteenth century to guard the land, especially Harwich Harbour, against invasion coming from the North Sea. Over the centuries it has been enlarged and has a labyrinth of passages but it was abandoned by the Army in 1957. It's now a museum administered by English Heritage. The large crater is almost certainly a relic of gravel extraction and removal, the smaller indentations are footings of extinct buildings. The dotted line on the seaward side is a series of concrete tank traps and the building at the end of the sandy road housed a searchlight. The large concrete block near the port radar is a two storeyed Second World War pill box.

European Gateway

On 19 December 1982 in the approach to Felixstowe Harbour, the ferry *European Gateway* collided with the sealink train ferry *Speedlink Vanguard*. From a crew of 36 and 34 passengers, six lives were lost when she flooded and capsized onto a mudbank. After reclamation the boat was sold and since has had several new names and owners.

Landguard Point looking north

Landguard Fort

The original parts of the fort are the bastions at the corners. After its initial construction the fort decayed and garrison morale was low. When the Civil War was declared in 1642 the soldiers chose the Parliamentarian side because Charles I owed them seven years' back pay and they were starving. Improvements were made but by 1672 conditions had deteriorated again. 'This place is in the most miserable condition of any fort in Europe' was the complaint at the start of the third Dutch War. The two grey buildings near the water's edge are the nineteenth century Darrell's Battery built to defend the harbour entrance. They appeared in the film 'The Sea Shall Not Have Them'. The overdue rebuilding of the fort was brought to a halt in 1867 when Colonel Tomline bought up large areas of Felixstowe and discovered his entitlement to levy a toll on materials brought across the shoreline to the fort. The tolls escalated, the War Office rebelled and an enquiry resulted in one final payment to Tomline and the abolition of the tolls. Tomline then turned his considerable wealth and energy to creating Felixstowe Port and bringing the railway to it, but contemporary reports state he was ever afterwards offensive to the officers of the fort whenever he came across them. The three low concrete block buildings housed searchlights in the Second World War.

Old Felixstowe

The fishtail pebble reinforcements at Cobbold's Point give a clue to the constant battle with the sea, but other battles and threats of battles have taken place along here. Just offshore lie the submerged remains of the Saxon Shore fort at Walton, established towards the end of the Roman occupation. During the First World War Brackenbury Fort was created along the clifftop but the guns were never fired at full charge for fear of bringing down the cliffs! Because of the Napoleonic Wars, Martello Towers were hastily erected along this stretch, one at the mouth of the Deben and one nearer Felixstowe ferry in Woodbridge Haven. An Armada Beacon was hoisted to commemorate the 400th anniversary of the sighting of the Spanish Armada.

Felixstowe town

The advent of the railway in 1877 added to Felixstowe's popularity as a holiday resort, as did the stay here of the Empress of Germany in 1891. The railway track from Landguard Common to Felixstowe Beach Station shows as a straight line parallel with the coast. The pier used to be 800 metres long (the second longest in England) with electric trams meeting the steamers from London and Great Yarmouth. Mrs Simpson stayed in Beach House during the 1936 abdication crisis but the house has since been demolished and a block of flats replaces it. The River Deben is in the background.

Beach huts

Along all accessible parts of the Suffolk coast beach huts abound. These particular huts are at Old Felixstowe but anywhere with road access within carrying distance for buckets and spades, books, tea making equipment and beach towels has at least one row of colourful bolt holes.

Felixstowe looking south-west

The sandy shallow knolls of the mouth of the River Deben (foreground) are a hazard for small boats entering Woodbridge Haven. In the distance the cranes of the container terminal have a reach of over 55 metres.

The community of Felixstowe Ferry

At the edge of what must be one of the most picturesquely sited golf courses in all England lies the small hamlet of Felixstowe Ferry. The operation of the foot ferry gives employment at weekends only but there are several boat repair yards and fishing boats based here. During the 1930s the wooden hull of a Supermarine Southampton flying boat was moored as a houseboat at the Ferry, then subsequently claimed by the RAF Museum.

Opposite: **Felixstowe Ferry and the mouth of the River Deben**

No longer can a bell be rung to summon the ferryman, instead and less picturesquely, a wooden board held high summons his services. All the river estuaries along the Suffolk Coast are heaven for small sailing boats.

Woodbridge

This picturesque small town is at the end of the Deben navigation. Deben is said to mean 'deep one' but the river is not very deep now as sailors will testify. The Tide Mill (centre picture) and its predecessors have been there since 1170; this one dates from 1793 and is made from ships' timbers.

Woodbridge Tide Mill

The Tide Mill ceased to grind grain in 1967 although the building was restored in 1976. It worked by allowing the tide to fill the pond, which is now a marina. As the tide outside fell, a pair of sluices were opened to turn an undershot wheel. The pond in the foreground was made in 1978 to provide sufficient water for demonstrations.

Woodbridge and the River Deben

Bawdsey Manor
Bawdsey Manor had been built in 1885 by stockbroker and Liberal Member of Parliament for South Suffolk, Sir Cuthbert Quilter but it was just another grand house until it was acquired by the Air Ministry in 1936.

Opposite: **Felixstowe Ferry looking towards Bawdsey**
At Bawdsey Manor Sir Robert Watson Watt lead a top secret team of scientists in developing early radar which became a significant factor in gaining victory in the Second World War.

Bawdsey looking south

Incredible now to think that Bloodhound Missiles were parked here in the 1970s during the Cold War on the site of a line of masts which were part of the Chain Home radar transmitters and receivers erected in the late 1930s. The last mast was dismantled in 2000, the present mast is smaller than the originals and is used by the Maritime Agency. Now a more peaceful use of the site involves the plastic coverings (showing white) enabling an early crop of vegetables, probably carrots, to grow on this light sandy soil.

Bawdsey Village
Suffolk's second lifeboat was installed here in 1801, Suffolk's first was Lowestoft in the same year. Nearby Alderton village is the start of the Heritage Coast Walk with 35 miles of (more or less) continuous footpath to Lowestoft.

Coastal erosion at Bawdsey

The Martello Towers were built to protect against *human* invasion but the *sea* invades by stealth where the coast is unprotected. Most of the East Anglian Martello towers are ovoid in shape, rather than round, thereby presenting a smaller surface area from a head-on attack from out at sea.

Barque *Endeavour* in Hollesley Bay

In 1988, to commemorate the bicentenary of European settlement in Australia, a replica of Captain James Cook's original three-masted barque of the same name was commissioned. Launched in 1994 the 32-metre-long vessel made a round the world trip and during her visit to the British Isles Mike Page was able to take this picture whilst she was in Hollesley Bay. She is now in the National Maritime Museum in Sydney, Australia.

Looking north-west

The shingle spit has been formed by the North Sea meeting the coastline at an angle which pushes the shingle and silt southwards to the mouth of a river where it is deposited. Over the centuries the spit has grown at a rate of approximately 14 yards per year.

Opposite: **Shingle Street looking north**

The mouth of the River Ore separates Shingle Street from Orford beach. This is one of the most isolated hamlets on the Suffolk Coast. The coastguard cottages are the white buildings to the right of picture. A few years ago Shingle Street was the subject of a BBC programme claiming that it may have been the site of a Second World War German invasion attempt since shipwrecked submariners were washed ashore there. This remains speculation. There was another tragedy in 1914 when five coastguards drowned when their boat capsized within sight of their homes. The hamlet was evacuated in 1940 when the army took over the area for battle training. The Martello Tower was used for target practice but a Wellington Bomber missed the target and bombed the Lifeboat Inn instead. The area has SSSI status.

Shingle Street looking south

Shingle Street is aptly named; it's the third largest deposit of shingle in the UK. Mounds of the stuff rise up on the spring tides and then disappear again.

Opposite: **Orford Beach and the River Ore**

The shifting sandbanks of Orford Haven present challenges to the leisure sailor. The Butley River joins the Ore just above Flybury Point, with Havergate Island in the distance.

Sailors beware

This sea monster is composed of sand and shingle in the mouth of the River Ore, but it creeps around to trap the unwary sailor.

The shingle spit at the mouth of the River Ore

The tip of the long shingle stretch of Orford Beach and the mouth of the River Ore look over to the complex of what is now H M Youth Custody and Detention Centre. But it was built in 1886 as the Hollesley Bay Colony to train young gentlemen who wished to settle in the Colonies. They learned about forestry, farming, surveying, building and carpentry. In 1906 it became a training centre for the unemployed, and a prison in 1939. A pilot used to be employed to guide commercial traffic along the Ore to Snape Maltings.

Lower Gull and the Butley River

Lower Gull is the reach in the river immediately before the mouth of the Butley River and opposite Dove Point on Havergate Island. A gull is a deep channel from which 'gully' derives.

Opposite: **Hollesley Bay Colony with the Butley River in the background**

Butley River looking towards Havergate Island

The Butley River flows into the Ore at the point where the triangle of Havergate Island can be picked out on the skyline in front of the Orford shingle bank. This is the wildest and remotest part of Suffolk, inaccessible by road. The derelict oyster beds were revitalised in the 1950s and there is a thriving Butley Orford Oysterage in Orford which has been run by the same family for over 50 years. Barges used to work up to Butley Mills.

Opposite: **Marsh patterns, Butley River**

The fantastic shapes and colours of the saltmarsh in winter can best be appreciated from overhead.

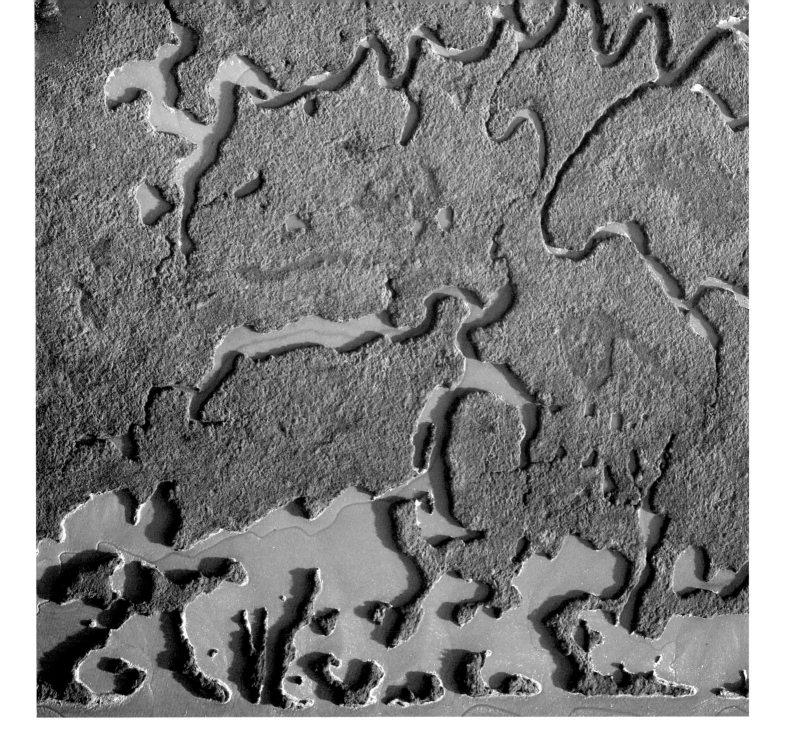

Havergate Island looking south

The island is now an RSPB Reserve and famous for the fact that in 1947 the first pair of avocets returned to breed, now there's a colony of 85-90 pairs, along with black-headed gulls, spoonbill and sandwich and common terns. Cuckold's Point is the near tip of the island with Dove Point opposite the mouth of the Butley River. Access to the island is by ferry from Orford Quay but prior arrangements have to be made with the RSPB. The island is protected from the sea by Orford Ness. It's difficult now to believe that in the 1800s a family lived here and grazed cattle but the area became flooded when a Second World War shell used in target practice destroyed accidentally one of the sluices. Its remoteness had until then made it a haven for smugglers.

Orford Ness looking north

This shingle spit has been extending south for centuries; it's an important landfall for migratory birds and has a large gull colony. There's been a lighthouse here since the sixteenth century and at one time had a female lighthouse keeper. The coast has eroded at least 5 metres in the last 2-3 years and there's concern that the present 99' high lighthouse eventually will be lost to the sea, as was an earlier light. The masts and white transmitter building in the background belong now to the BBC World Service. Placed in a radial pattern they and the gaunt building next to them belonged originally to the Cobra Mist era. Cobra Mist was an Anglo-American initiative of 1972. It was an early warning device designated as a Radio Research Station surrounded by a high wire fence. In the distance is Sizewell Nuclear Power Station.

Orford Ness lighthouse looking west
Looking across the water of Stony Ditch and the River Ore towards Orford Castle and Church.

Opposite:
Masts at Orford Ness
Part of the Cobra Mist era, apparently these 60' high masts became redundant after eighteen months!

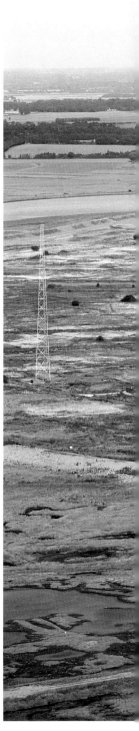

Orford Ness looking south

The River Ore runs to the right of picture. The peninsula which is Orford Beach is divided at this southern point by Stony Ditch. Stony Ditch peters out, the Ore becomes the Alde and Orford Beach joins to the main Suffolk coast by a thin strip of shingle at Slaughden next to Aldeburgh. In 1913 the War Department drained the site and made airfields for the Experimental Flying Section where parachutes, aerial photographs, bomb sights and camouflage were developed and ballistic experiments took place. The Atomic Weapons Research Establishment made provision for atomic bomb testing during the 1950s during the Cold War. The 'pagodas' were test cells, part of the atomic bomb research.

The Black Tower
Erected in 1928 by the Royal Aircraft Establishment, Farnborough, to be an experimental rotating loop navigational beacon, it's now an elevated viewing and display area. Wheatears and ringed plovers nest nearby.

The Pagodas

The 'Pagodas' were built to test triggers for nuclear warheads in the 1960s. They were constructed in such a way that if they exploded accidentally then the roof would collapse in upon the building thereby containing everything within.

Orford

Following the construction of Orford Castle in the twelfth century the marshes were drained and the port of Orford established. Ships sailed from the quay to the Siege of Calais in 1346. Orford's mediaeval prosperity was built on exporting wool and fishing but centuries of shingle build up has destroyed the port. Today the only boats from Orford Quay are fishing boats for the smoked fish and oyster trade – the oysters are harvested in Butley Creek – and small craft and ferries crossing to Orford Beach (National Trust) and Havergate (RSPB). St Bartholomew's church, built in the same century as the Castle, was the venue for the first ever performance of Benjamin Britten's 'Noye's Fludde' in 1958.

Orford Castle

Only the keep and two towers of Orford Castle remain. Built by Henry II (murderer by proxy of Thomas à Becket) and subsequently occupied by generations of the ruthless Bigod family, it was intended to discourage raiders from the sea. Originally it was surrounded by several 90' high towers which served as landmarks.

Opposite:
Orford looking west

The River Alde and the sea

In the stretch of water between Hollesley Bay and Aldeburgh, the River Ore becomes the River Alde and none can say with any certainty where exactly this point is! Originally they were two separate rivers but the shingle ridge built southwards until the mouth of the Alde was blocked at the hamlet of Slaughden (Slorden). Slaughden has been claimed by the sea within the last hundred years; for several decades in the nineteenth century a life-boat was based here until coastal erosion caused the station to be abandoned in 1890.

Aldeburgh looking north

Aldeburgh with Thorpeness village and Sizewell Nuclear Power Station in the background. The original Aldeburgh Harbour lay to the north between the present-day town and the Ness.

Opposite: **Aldeburgh's Martello Tower**

The last and largest in a line of 103 Martello Towers stretching from Seaford in Sussex. Part of the moat remains. All threat of Napoleonic Invasion being over, this particular one has been converted into a holiday property and rented out by the Landmark Trust. The River Alde provides safe sailing for small craft.

Safe Sailing

Safe sailing at Aldeburgh, safe that is unless sailors are intrepid enough to venture along the Alde/Ore and out to sea across the sandbanks.

Opposite: **Aldeburgh**

What remains of Aldeburgh is only half of the original town, the rest has been lost to the sea. Shipbuilding was one of the town's major industries (Francis Drake's *Golden Hind* was built here) and ship auctions used to be held in the Parish Church until the port silted up. The churchyard contains the graves of Benjamin Britten, Peter Pears and Imogen Holst as well as a memorial to all the lifeboatmen lost at sea over the years. Dr Elizabeth Garret Anderson, both the country's first woman doctor and first woman Mayor of Aldeburgh, was born in the town. And 'Owlbarrow', the setting for Kathleen Hale's *Orlando the Marmalade Cat* series of children's books, is a thinly disguised Aldeburgh.

Aldeburgh looking west
Thames barges worked up to the Aldeburgh Brick Works at the clay pit behind the town.

Opposite: **The Moot Hall**
The Moot Hall (mid picture) was in the middle of the town before erosion from the sea. It was the Town Hall and prison for centuries and is now the Museum. The Model Yacht Pond to the left of the War Memorial has next to it a model of 'Snooks', the pet dog of Patrick and Nora Acheson, both well loved Aldeburgh doctors. The statue was stolen recently but a copy from the original casting has replaced it. Fishermen's huts string along the shingle and the lifeboat *Freddie Cooper* is launched from the beach.

Snape, end of navigation

Long before Snape was put on the map with the Concert Hall converted from Maltings, evidence of an Anglo Saxon burial ground was uncovered in The Sandlings, the dry sandy heathland of this special area of Suffolk. In 1862 the first excavations were made and the rivets of a Viking ship were found. Reconstruction led to the discovery of a whole burial ship and human remains both cremated and interred were found. This was decades before the better known ship burial at nearby Sutton Hoo was unearthed. The Maltings closed in 1960 but the Aldeburgh Festival soon took over the building and converted it to a Concert Hall. It suffered a fire in 1969 but was rebuilt in record time. In 1979 the adjacent barley store was converted to the Britten-Pears Music School and small shops, art galleries, sculpture and eating places are contained within the complex.

The River Alde looking towards the sea

Thames barges used to come along this stretch of tidal river up to Snape. Although the sea is only five miles away in a direct line, because Aldeburgh Harbour silted up, the mouth of the River Alde is now approximately 20 miles away at Orford Haven! The quaint church at Iken stands idyllically on the near promontory (right) with a wooded backdrop. Snape village is in the foreground to the left, Snape Maltings to the right.

Beach Sculpture

Maggi Hambling's controversial sculpture is a memorial to Lowestoft-born composer and long time Aldeburgh resident Benjamin Britten. The scallop shell, installed 2003, bears the inscription 'I hear those voices that will not be drowned' – a line spoken by fisherman Peter Grimes in Britten's opera of the same name. The line originates in George Crabbe's poem 'The Borough' about a fishing town and its inhabitants. Crabbe was born in Aldeburgh 1754. The steel 4 tonne sculpture was locally made by foundrymen father and son Sam and Dennis Pegg. It stands 12ft high and will withstand winds of 100mph.

Thorpeness, House in the Clouds

At Thorpeness all is not as it might seem. The 100' high House in the Clouds is a water tower, the windmill was imported from Aldringham and stands over a well from which it pumped water to the House in the Clouds. A second water tower resembles a Tudor Gatehouse.

Thorpeness

The Tudor-style gatehouse cum Water Tower.

Opposite: **Thorpeness looking west**

Around 1908 Glencairn Stuart Ogilvie created the mock-Tudor holiday village. A small exit to the North Sea was dammed up and the Hundred River diverted: the 90 acre mere is no deeper than 3′ anywhere and is full of islands in which a child in a boat can let imagination rip. JM Barrie was a friend of Stuart Ogilvie and the scene has much in common with that in *Peter Pan*. There is a coastal road of sorts linking Thorpeness with Aldeburgh. The area is devoid of main coast roads thereby avoiding ribbon development.

Looking north towards Sizewell
The Ness is being eroded by the sea. Sizewell Hall Conference Centre and Home Farm are dwarfed by Sizewell Nuclear Power Station.

Opposite: **Ness House, Thorpeness**
Lovely sea views and hopefully, in the decades to come if coastal erosion becomes under control, more view and less sea.

Sizewell B dominates the landscape

Sizewell Village

This small fishing village and haven for smugglers, was changed forever with the advent of the Nuclear Power Station in 1961. Sizewell A stands to the left of picture and is a First Generation Magnox Reactor. Sizewell B (with dome) was the first Pressurised Water Reactor begun in 1987 and taking seven years to build. Radiation levels surrounding both installations are checked frequently. In 2005 plans for Sizewell C had been shelved, now we wait to see. On the seafront there's a café called 'Sizewell T'… get it?

Minsmere RSPB reserve looking north west

In 1940 the Minsmere Levels were flooded to protect against invasion and the area was declared a Prohibited Zone. In 1947 avocets returned to breed here as they did at Havergate Island. The RSPB negotiated the lease of 1500 acres to establish the Nature Reserve which opened in 1949. The large areas and brackish lagoons and shallow islands (scrapes) were created from land drained a century earlier for grazing pasture on the site of Minsmere Broad. The Broad had occurred when the mouth of the River Min became blocked. The scrapes provide ideal breeding conditions for the avocet; 100 pairs are now present. Marsh harriers, bittern and otters now frequent the Reserve. Salinity in the pools is controlled to 2 per cent salt to encourage crustacea to feed, which in turn provide a food supply for the bird population.

**Minsmere RSPB
reserve looking west**

**Minsmere RSPB
reserve looking east**
The group of coastguard cottages
are on the horizon top left.

Coastguard Cottages at Dunwich Heath

In previous centuries the coastguards stationed here were fully occupied trying to catch smugglers. This whole coastal area of sandy heathland is known as 'The Sandlings'.

Coastguard Cottages

The National Trust rents out the cottages for holidays. At the end of the row stands the former gun battery and Observation Post offering today's visitors a wonderful view out to sea. There's also a Field Study Centre and on the ground floor is the facility without which a National Trust property would be incomplete – a Tea Shop.

The Sandlings at Dunwich Heath
Gorse and heather thrive in the acid sandy soil, as do the Corsican and Scots pines planted along with broadleaved trees by the Forestry Commission in the 1920s to form Dunwich Forest.

Opposite: **Dunwich Forest**
Rideways, here carpeted in gorse, separate the blocks of pines allowing greater accessibility to the trees. The Rideways are fire breaks.

Dunwich Beach
The foreground restaurant building is reckoned to serve the best fish and chips anywhere. The remains of the cliffs, here as elsewhere along this stretch of coast, still are very much at risk from the sea.

Ecclesiastical remains

Dunwich was once a thriving port trading with the Baltic Sea ports and with Scandinavian countries. Over the last eight centuries four hundred houses and several churches have been lost to the sea. The first church had been submerged by the time Domesday Book was compiled. In the early thirteenth century Dunwich was the sixth greatest town in England but fierce storms in the fourteenth century blocked the harbour mouth which led to the rapid decline of the town. It is estimated that the sea has encroached at least a quarter of a mile since 1587. Seven successive parish churches have fallen over the cliffs, the last in 1922 leaving exposed graves and a couple of headstones in the undergrowth. For all the good it did Dunwich in subsequent centuries, Magna Carta (1215) granted the town (city) self government and the right to a Mayor. Part of the ruined Franciscan Friary and part of the leper hospital remain. Until the Reform Act of 1832 Dunwich was a 'rotten boro' – it sent two Members of Parliament to represent a non-existent population. The unlikely legend that the bells of Dunwich churches can be heard out at sea prompted sceptical travel writer Mark Wallington to say 'If you've had enough Adnams* you can hear them off Southwold as well'.

*Adnams Southwold Brewery

Dunwich looking north

The beach stretches to the entrance of Southwold Harbour whilst the vulnerability of the coast and the land behind it is plain to see.

Westwood Marshes looking north-east toward Southwold

Probably this is the largest area of uninterrupted freshwater reed beds in the UK. Bitterns and marsh harriers nest within the reeds which are harvested for thatching. Hen harriers, merlin and the short-eared owl are regular visitors, with occasional sightings of a buzzard.

Dingle Marshes
This picture was taken after the shingle bank breach in December 2005. The inland strip of water parallel with the coast is the Dunwich river on its way into Southwold Harbour.

Walberswick

Walberswick's real prosperity was in the fourteenth century when butter, bacon, corn and fish were traded from Walberswick – fishing boats travelled as far as the Faroes and Iceland. But a hundred years ago prosperity of a different kind came to the hamlet when artists Philip Wilson Steer, Stanley Spencer and Charles Rennie Mackintosh came here to paint. Many of the houses are now holiday cottages. The Dunwich River assumed a new course, seen here behind the marshes, when Dunwich harbour became silted up, it now joins the River Blyth near the harbour entrance. A capstan used to stand on the old pier to help the ships into harbour over the shingle bar. During the seventeenth century Walberswick along with Covehithe and Corton churches gained permission to pull down the old and rebuild a smaller church because the congregation was diminishing.

Walberswick and the River Blyth

The River Blyth Chain Ferry Company operated a vehicle-carrying pontoon ferry across the river 1885–1942, sometimes it sank mid-stream. There remains a foot ferry between Walberswick and Southwold, the oldest rowed ferry in East Anglia. The expression 'drumming up support' originated in Southwold where the Corporation sent a drummer round the streets to rustle up all available help in digging out the harbour entrance when it had become blocked yet again. The annual Crabbing Festival is held here each July, the entrant catching the largest crab in 90 minutes is the winner.

Blythburgh looking toward Southwold

The magnificence of the tidal broad expanse of the River Blyth can be appreciated from the A12 road (foot of picture). There were plans to make the river navigable as far as Halesworth and in 1761 the first keel took coal to the town. But the river kept silting up, at one time it was said that at low tide carriages were able to drive across the river from Southwold to Walberswick. Seagoing boats had to unload their cargoes into the wherry *Good Intent* offshore (kept especially for the purpose) because of the sand bar at the harbour entrance.

Walberswick looking north

Yellow oilseed rape flowers brighten the landscape for about three weeks in May. The bridge across the River Blyth was previously a railway swing bridge; the route of the single track still can be seen. The Southwold Railway ran from 1879–1929 with stations at Walberswick, Blythburgh, Wenhaston and Halesworth. Southwold and Reydon are mid picture. Easton Broad and marshes (showing brown with reed growth) and Benacre Broad further north are all at risk from invasion by the sea. Looking north, Benacre Ness is prominent, then the coastline recedes to Lowestoft on the horizon.

Opposite: **Mud patterns on the Blyth Estuary**
Large flocks of birds (the white patches) roost and feed on the mud at low tide, but sailors beware!

Opposite: The River Blyth and Southwold Harbour
The freshest fish anywhere is sold from the fishermen's huts along the river at Southwold.

Fast Ride
Take a speedboat ride out to sea from Southwold Harbour.

Southwold looking north towards Benacre

In 1672 the inhabitants of Southwold stood on the cliffs to watch the Battle of Sole Bay fought against the Dutch. It was England's first real threat of invasion since 1066. The cannons lined up on Gun Hill were said to have been put there originally to discourage pirates. The pier was rebuilt in 2001 and contains an ingenious (and slightly rude) water clock. Amber is sometimes found on the beach – the fossilised resin from prehistoric pine trees. Where the concrete sea defences end, the erosion begins.

Southwold and Reydon

Buss Creek in diminished form flows along the northern edge of Southwold, it now empties into the harbour upriver of the footbridge. A buss was a square rigged herring smack mentioned in Samuel Pepys' Diary (1660s). Southwold landmarks include the lighthouse (1890), the church whose Victorian stained-glass windows were blown out during the Second World War, and Adnams Brewery whose horses and drays until very recently were a common sight in the town. Southwold's neighbour, Reydon, made the news in 2001 when a vulture escaped from a zoo and sat for 6 days on the Vicarage roof – an avian equivalent of Seeking Sanctuary?

Southwold

The 101' lighthouse dominates the town. The Sailors' Reading Room along the front was set up in 1864 to lure sailors and fishermen away from the pubs and other temptations of life onshore. Today it's more of a museum and well worth a visit.

Reydon looking north-east

St Felix Girls' School is in the foreground.

Southwold Pier

The pier was built in 1899 to serve the Belle steamers which ran pleasure trips between Great Yarmouth and London Bridge. Reopened in 2001; winning the 'Pier of the Year' award in 2002. Here Southwold lifeboat, an Atlantic 75 B class rigid inflatable the *Leslie Tranmer* which has been in service since 1998, is showing what it can do. Southwold lifeboat the *Mary Scott* was one of the 19 lifeboats at the Dunkirk Evacuation June 1940.

Rough seas Southwold
Winter storms have caused much of the erosion along the coast.

A barge unloading sea defence materials
Large stones imported from Scandinavia break the force of the waves.

Beach regeneration
Sand is sucked from the seabed and pumped on to the beach to build up the beach levels.

Easton Bavents

This picture was taken in 2000.

Easton Bavents
Five years later in 2005.

Easton Broad

Easton, Covehithe and Benacre Broads (all having SSSI status) are experiencing increased coastal erosion. High tides coinciding with gale force winds cause increased swell which in turn leads to faster erosion. Shingle spits are breached and water escapes from the Broads. The incursion of salt water into the freshwater reed beds is reducing the quality and vigour of the reed. In 1986 a medieval rudder was dredged up here in what was once a Viking estuary.

Opposite: **Easton Bavents – one man's sea defences**

For several years Peter Boggis has been placing lorry loads of clay soil at the base of the cliff near his home in an attempt to halt erosion. His actions are controversial especially since the dumping has been done without planning permission but it highlights homeowners' distress in all areas where their property is likely to fall into the sea. Residents of clifftop homes in Happisburgh, Norfolk are hoping that some government help is on the way to resolve their similar situation. Easton Bavents gets it unusual name from the fact that the land was a tun (Old English for an enclosure), and this was the eastern enclosure belonging to Thomas de Bavents from Normandy.

Covehithe Broad

The shingle spit offers barely any protection. Covehithe Church is in the background. John de Cove had a harbour here in the fourteenth century where goods for his estate were unloaded.

Opposite: **Covehithe Church in sea fog**

Covehithe Church

The metalled road to the beach comes to an abrupt halt. The halt gets more abrupt year by year, Covehithe is fast crumbling into the sea. Fifty years ago Mike Page was a young boy and his passion was fishing. He and a friend came often to Covehithe. There was a bungalow called 'Four Winds' and a Gun Emplacement along the cliff at least half a mile seawards from where the road ends today, the Coastguard Lookout already had been washed away. The massive fifteenth century church used to serve three hundred parishioners but the population dwindled, the church became too big, was dismantled, and a smaller one built inside its shell using the original materials. The tower was left to serve as a landmark.

Benacre Broad after a breach

Opposite: **Benacre Broad**
Attempts have been made to build a protective clay wall at the inland end of the broad to protect the reed beds from the incursion of salt water.

Benacre erosion
1994.

Benacre erosion
2006.

Death by salt water

Benacre Pumping Station

The Hundred River is pumped out to the sea. There are many Hundred Rivers or Hundred Streams in East Anglia – a Hundred was a Saxon parish. At the start of the Second World War gravel was extracted here to build nearby Ellough Airfield.

Kessingland looking north

The Suffolk Coast and Heath path runs along the beach. Holiday camps and caravan sites start here and continue along the coast for approximately fifty miles to Weybourne in Norfolk – one result of having a Coast Road. East Point aka Lowestoft Ness, aka Ness Point, with its new wind turbine is the most easterly point in Britain.

Kessingland Wildlife Park
Giraffes in Suffolk? These are in Kessingland's Wildlife Park and Mike Page couldn't resist including them.

Opposite: **Kessingland**
Longshore drift has resulted in the build-up of the beach. There used to be four lifeboats at Kessingland and another at Benacre – an indication of the treacherous nature of this coast.

Kessingland looking west on a foggy morning

Kessingland looking towards Lowestoft
Ness Point on the horizon.

Erosion continues near Kessingland

Pakefield

Fishing huts and fishing boats on the beach. Many of the older houses have been washed into the sea. There's an old saying about Pakefield 'The older it gets the smaller it gets'. The curious church shares a tower but has two naves – it was once two churches with two parishes worshipping separately. There was a vigorous Beach Colony here, as at Kessingland, and along many stretches of the Suffolk and Norfolk coasts. The Beach Companies pre-dated the lifeboat service and the members made their livings from saving lives at sea and salvaging wrecks – hopefully in that order!

The Centre for Environment, Fisheries and Aquaculture (CEFAS)

There's been a Fisheries Laboratory here since the research station (the first and principal of three in the country) opened in 1902. The original cream-washed premises are the former Grand Hotel, with a new extension. The lab was set up originally to research declining fish stocks. All aspects of marine, coastal and freshwater environments are monitored with particular attention to fishing, pollution, disease and climate change upon fish populations and the aquatic ecosystem.

CEFAS *Endeavour*

Endeavour was launched in 2002 as a Fisheries Research vessel. In 2004 she took part in a dramatic life-saving rescue when one of two men in a small yacht had a suspected heart attack when off the Isles of Scilly. The yacht radioed for help and when *Endeavour* reached it the man was taken on board and then transferred to hospital by helicopter. His life was saved. At the time there were nine scientists from Lowestoft on board undertaking scientific research on mackerel plankton.

Lowestoft looking north

The harbour is an artificial cut, the result of several attempts between 1820 and 1840 to break through the spit to the sea. Once the port of Lowestoft was established no longer did ships have to use Great Yarmouth to bring in goods for Norwich. In an act of corporate vandalism the fishing village (right of harbour) was demolished and industry was allowed to secure prime sites along the seafront. Until recently shipbuilding and repairing were main industries but they, like the fishing industry, have just about gone. The once busy fish dock is to the right of the harbour entrance as is the area devoted to fabricating accommodation platforms for the North Sea oil industry. The newest landmark is the wind turbine at Ness Point, the tallest in Britain (126 metres, 413 feet) erected 2006.

Lowestoft lifeboat

The Spirit of Lowestoft 47′ Tyne Class lifeboat returning to Lowestoft. With a top speed of 18 knots and a range of 100 miles the 25 tonne boat is equipped with the latest navigational and communication aids. The figures on the hull 47-0-20 represent the length of the boat (47 feet) the material from which she is made (0 = steel) and 20 (the 20th boat in this class).

Lowestoft Harbour

Much of the leisure traffic coming into Lowestoft harbour makes for the new enlarged marina (left) next to the prestigious Royal Norfolk and Suffolk Yacht Club. Many craft come across the North Sea from Holland and Germany during the summer months. The bascule bridge across the river allows larger craft into the Inner Harbour and Lake Lothing; smaller boats with a shallow draught can then get access to The Broads through Mutford Lock.

Lowestoft Air Show crowds

The Air Show has become an annual summer event. The most dramatic incident so far happened in August 2002 when an RAF Harrier suffered an engine failure accompanied by a loud bang. All displays take place over the sea, the pilot was able to jettison his canopy, bale out and land unhurt in the sea – all witnessed by a large crowd. The aircraft was recovered a week later.

Lowestoft cloudscape

Sea fog around the wind turbine

Lake Lothing

In the foreground stands the Wherry Hotel with its elegant Edwardian architecture, Oulton Broad Yacht Station is to the right. Mutford Lock is a double sea lock, there are two tides arriving from opposite directions about an hour and a half apart. The first is from the sea through Lake Lothing, the second comes in from Great Yarmouth via the River Waveney and Oulton Dyke. On the 'Salt Side' new enterprises are revitalising this part of the harbour which was once so busy with commercial traffic. The tall white grain silo is still in use; grain is moved out by ship. The huge former Brooke Marine premises are to the right at the bend in the river. In the 1950s Brooke Marine had an order to build what they thought were fishing trawlers for Russia. Later these boats were spotted during a NATO exercise with surveillance aerials all over them! The railway bridge in the foreground and the newer road bridge upriver of it work in unison to open when access to or exit from Mutford Lock is required On the horizon stand wind turbine legs awaiting transportation by barge to Scroby Wind Farm. A new marina lies opposite the Lowestoft Cruising Club (centre picture).

Lowestoft wind turbine looking north
The UK's tallest wind turbine; pity its landward surroundings aren't more inspiring.

Opposite: **Lowestoft and Oulton Broad**

Lowestoft High Light

The High Light (to distinguish it from the Low Light which used to stand closer to the sea and further south) was installed in 1874 but a light had been here since the 1600s. Fuelled originally by paraffin, then gas and now electricity, the fifty-nine feet high light stands one hundred and twenty three feet above sea level. In the foreground are the poles where the fishing nets were hung to dry after being treated with cutch, a preservative solution derived from oak bark. The cream-painted red-roofed buildings were where the 'beatsters' used to mend the nets and where stood the tanks in which the nets were immersed in the cutch to counteract the damaging effects of the salt water.

Opposite: **Lowestoft looking north**

This wonderful overall view shows the entrance to Yarmouth Harbour and the bulge of the North Denes with the expanse of Breydon Water just below the horizon.

Excelsior sailing off Corton

The 77' ketch *Excelsior* LT472. Lowestoft built in 1921, the Excelsior Trust of Lowestoft brought her back from Scandinavia and restored her in 1982. She has taken part in the Tall Ships Race. These fishing smacks (of which there were hundreds) were a common sight in Lowestoft harbour until the Second World War. The ochre tan sails on the main and mizzen masts must have been a magnificent sight as they set out for the fishing grounds. All Lowestoft fishing boats bore the letters LT (the first and last letter of their home port)and their particular number. When Lowestoft had a fishing industry often there were a hundred and more fishing boats tied up at Lowestoft and Yarmouth from harbours all up the east coast (GY = Grimsby, YH = Yarmouth, PD = Peterhead etc). Taking this picture was particularly poignant for Mike Page as his father, who died at sea during the War when Mike was only two years old, joined the fishing fleet in 1919 working his way up from cook to skipper by 1927 as was the accepted route on trawlers.

Sea fog at Corton

The swirling fog disguises some of Corton's crumbling cliffs. Large stones have been positioned at their base to break the force of the waves.

Damage to Corton sea wall February 2004

And sea wall repairs September 2003

Sea wall repairs complete

Corton
Flying saucers have not landed. A much more down to earth subject – they're part of the new Corton Sewage Works!

Waves pound the defences between Corton and Hopton

Hopton in winter
Perhaps not the best time to take a holiday here!

Hopton looking north-west
Once a small fishing village, the church burned down in 1865 and sensibly was rebuilt further inland. In the old churchyard is a large rusty anchor: 'anchor swiping' – trawling for anchors for salvage – used to be almost as lucrative as smuggling in this village. About half of Hopton now comprises holiday camps. Hopton has moved – not literally – but the village was in Suffolk until the county boundaries were reorganised a few years ago.

Hopton looking south into Suffolk

The railway line seen here at Hopton ran the short distance between Great Yarmouth and Lowestoft but closed in 1970. The line of the track still can be picked out roughly parallel with the A12 road. The A12 is never far from the coast the entire length of 'Silly Suffolk', except that silly is a corruption of 'selig' meaning fortunate or blessed, and who could argue with that!